This book belongs to:

這本書屬於：

Bearific's® Chinese New Year

棒棒熊的中國新年

Written & Illustrated by: Katelyn Lonas

作者與繪圖：婁開倫

It was a new year in Berrytown.

草莓鎮的新年。

Bearific® was super excited for Chinese New Year!

棒棒熊好興奮中國新年快到了！

2 二

Every year Berrytown holds a huge celebration!

每年草莓鎮都有一個大慶典！

3 三

Bearific® called her friend Mei to see if she wanted to go together to the Chinese New Year Celebration.

棒棒熊打給她的朋友小美並問她想不想一起去看中國新年慶典。

4 四

Mei told Bearific® she would have loved to go, but the Mayor this year can't afford to host a big celebration for Chinese New Year.

小美說今年草莓鎮不會主辦中國新年慶典，因為沒有經費。

5 五

Bearific® couldn't believe what she heard! They couldn't just cancel the Chinese New Year Celebration! It was a tradition!

棒棒熊無法相信她的耳朵！他們不能取消中國新年慶典！這是一個傳統！

6 六

Bearific® and Mei decided to meet at Berra's Cafe.

棒棒熊和小美決定在草莓鎮的咖啡店見面。

7 七

Once Bearific® arrived at Berra's Cafe, she spotted Mei waiting inside.

棒棒熊走進咖啡店，她看到小美已經在裡面等她了。

8 八

They ordered some berry tea.

他們叫了一些水果茶.

9 九

Bearific® and Mei were brainstorming ideas to save the Chinese New Year Celebration.

棒棒熊和小美在想她們如何來拯救中國新年慶典。

After a while of thinking, they came up with a plan!

然後她們想到了一個計畫！

Bearific® and Mei decided to host an event and see if any other bear fairies in Berrytown would like to help out.

棒棒熊和小美準備主辦一個活動會來看熊熊仙子們有什麼好主意。

12 十二

Bearific® and Mei posted about their plan on social media.

棒棒熊和小美用網路來公佈她們的活動會消息。

13 十三

I want to help!!

我要幫忙!

They got lots of support and volunteers from bear fairies!

好多熊熊仙子都支持並參與!

14 十四

Bearific® and Mei posted a list of items they need for the Chinese New Year Celebration!

棒棒熊和小美告訴大家中國新年慶典需要些什麼！

15 十五

Next, they flew to
Berra's Mall.

接著他們飛去草莓
鎮的購物中心。

16 十六

Bearific® went to buy red pockets and some lanterns.

棒棒熊去買紅包和燈籠。

17 十七

Mei went to buy dumplings,
meatballs, and egg rolls.

小美去買餃子，
獅子頭和春捲。

18 十八

After they finished shopping, Bearific® and Mei decided to start setting up the day before Chinese New Year.

她們買完了年貨並準備在除夕夜來佈置。

19 十九

February 十一

			11 十一			

A few days later. It was February 11th and the day before Chinese New Year.

很快的除夕在二月十一日就到來了。

20 二十

Bearific® and Mei started to set up and get everything ready for Chinese New Year.

棒棒熊和小美開始佈置慶典的現場。

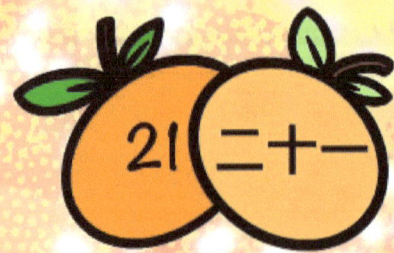

21 二十一

Other bear fairies in Berrytown started to show up to help set up.

熊熊仙子們都來幫忙。

22 二十二

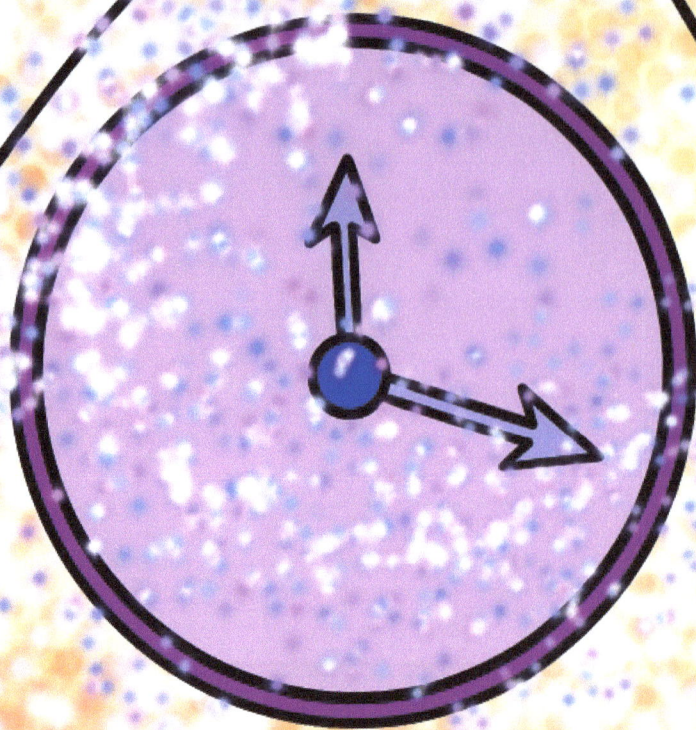

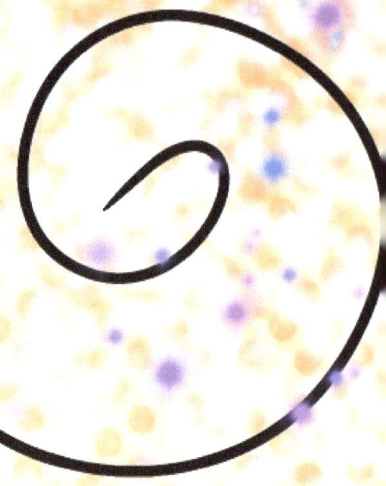

After hours of hard work, they finished setting up. All the bear fairies were excited for tomorrow!

幾個小時後，終於一切都就緒。大家都期待中國新年的到來。

23 二十三

The next day was finally
Chinese New Year!

明天就是中國新
年了!

24 二十四

Everyone in Berrytown gathered together to eat Chinese food and celebrate the new year!

草莓鎮的熊熊們齊聚一堂慶祝中國新年！

25 二十五

There was even a dragon parade with fireworks!

有舞龍舞獅遊行和煙火表演!

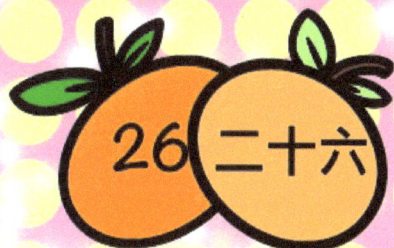

26 二十六

Older Bear fairies were giving out red pockets and watching the little ones playing firecrackers !

小熊熊仙子們開心的拿到紅包並一邊放著鞭炮。

27 二十七

Bearific® and Mei were having so much fun!

棒棒熊和小美玩的好開心!

They were so happy to celebrate the new year with everyone in Berrytown!

能和全鎮的熊熊仙子們一起慶祝中國新年是再開心也不過的事情了。

29 二十九

Red Pocket

紅包

- Red pockets are meant to bring good luck for the new year.
- Red pockets contain brand new dollar bills inside.
- You should place the red pocket under your pillow for protection and good luck.

LUCK

福

- 紅包是好運氣的象徵。
- 紅包要包新錢。
- 紅包要放在你的枕頭下面。

2021 is the year of the OX.

二零二一年是牛年

Fun Facts

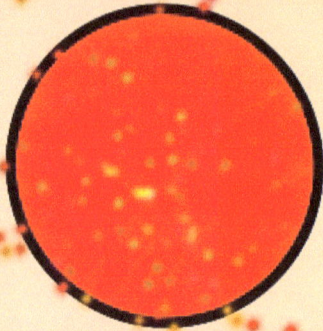

Red is a lucky color for Chinese New Year, it symbolizes happiness, success, and good fortune.

Tangerines (ju-zhi) are known for good fortune because of its pronunciation.

8 (ba) is the luckiest number for Chinese because of its pronunciation. It is a sign for wealth and prosperity.

有趣的傳統

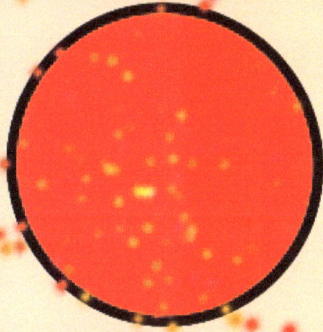

紅色是幸運的顏色。它代表快樂，成功，和好運氣。

橘子代表吉利

八是一個最幸運的數字。它代表繁榮和豐盛。

About Chinese New Year

- was around for over 3,500 years
- Chinese New Year is based on lunar new year which fluctuates every year
- is the time of bringing family together
- houses are cleaned before new year to rid them of inauspicious breaths, that might have collected during the previous year
- each year has a new zodiac animal which rotates between zodiac the rat, ox, tiger, rabbit, dragon, snake, horse, sheep, monkey, rooster, dog or pig
- lasts for 15 days

關於中國新年

- 有三千五百年的歷史
- 中國新年是農曆年
- 中國新年是家人團圓的日子
- 過年前要大掃除來去霉氣
- 中國傳統有十二生肖：鼠，牛，虎，兔，龍，蛇，馬，羊，猴，雞，狗和豬
- 中國新年會持續十五天

Draw a design on the red pocket and color it!

在紅包上畫圖樣!

Color the dragon!

給龍上色！

Check out other Bearific® books!
棒棒熊系列的書!

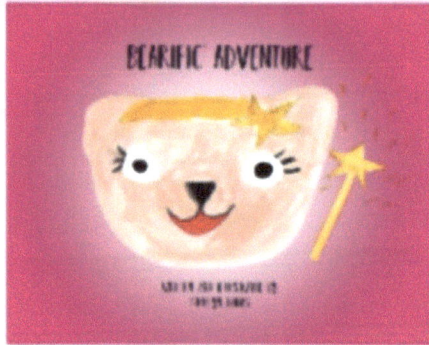
BEARIFIC ADVENTURE

BEARIFIC'S OCEAN ADVENTURE
WRITTEN & ILLUSTRATED BY KATELYN LONAS

BEARIFIC'S RAINFOREST ADVENTURE
WRITTEN & ILLUSTRATED BY: KATELYN LONAS

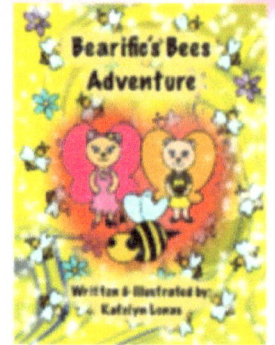
Bearific's Bees Adventure
Written & Illustrated by: Katelyn Lonas

Bearific's Cupcake Adventure
Written & Illustrated by: Katelyn Lonas

Bearific's Fashion Adventure

Bearific's Garden Adventure

Bearific's Ice Skating Adventure

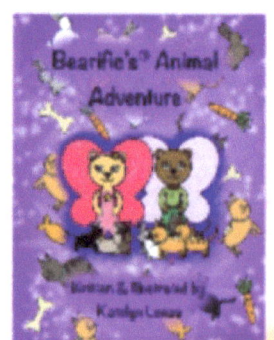
Bearific's Animal Adventure

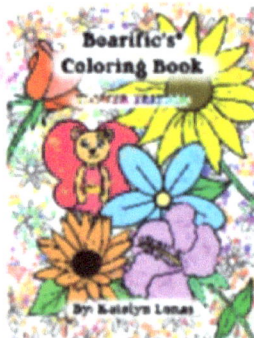
Bearific's Coloring Book

Bearific's Coloring Book

Bearific's Coloring Book

Bearific's Flower Mystery

Bearific's Pumpkin Mystery

BEARIFIC®

remember to: 記得要：

Believe 相信

Dream 夢想

Achieve 實現

Katelyn Lonas

Katelyn is a 14 year old who resides in Southern California. Katelyn loves to encourage others to always believe in themselves and chase after their dreams! She started writing and illustrating her first book at age 9 and then published 14 more books. She hopes you enjoy this book and learned some fun Chinese New Year facts. Thank you for reading Bearific's® Chinese New Year and be ready for more books to come!

— Katelyn

婁開倫

婁開倫今年十四歲。她住在加州。她鼓勵小朋友有夢想並努力實現他們的目標。她九歲開始寫作畫畫並出版她的第一本書。婁開倫現在出版了十五本書。她希望你們喜歡這本棒棒熊的中國新年。更希望大家去看看她其它系列的書籍。

— 婁開倫